WHAT TO BE?

By Meredith Powell and Gail Yokubinas

Illustrations by Richard Mlodock

CHILDRENS PRESS, CHICAGO

In memory of Mom, and for Dad, with special thanks to Mr. Ray Ziegler.

Copyright © 1972 by Regensteiner Publishing Enterprises, Inc. All rights reserved. Published simultaneously in Canada. Printed in the United States of America.

Library of Congress Catalog Card Number: 77-178497

1 2 3 4 5 6 7 8 9 10 11 12 13 14 15 16 17 18 19 20 21 22 23 24 25 R 75 74 73 72

Woe is me!
Woe is me!
What to be?
What to be?

An artist dreaming color schemes,
A seamstress sewing tucks and seams?
A nurse with soothing, loving hands?
A pilot seeking far-off lands?

Or maybe I should act on stage
In plays with sad or funny scenes.
It might be fun to write a book,
Or articles for magazines.

Would I be content to be
A wife and raise a family?
Or would I rather sail the sea,
Explore the world, be fancy-free?

Woe is me!
Woe is me!
What to be?
What to be?

I might be an oceanographer,
Or how about a court stenographer?
Could I be a choreographer?
Or a famous child photographer?

Maybe I could dance the lead
In music shows on ice!
Or be a prima ballerina
With grace and form precise.

Oh, why can't I be all of these?
However can I pick?
With all these possibilities,
To choose one is a trick.

Woe is me!
Woe is me!
What to be?
What to be?

A rugged lady lumberjack,
A chef who makes a good flapjack?
A concert pianist, self-taught?
A moon-bound lady astronaut?

A plumber, a drummer,
A folk guitar strummer?
A daring sky diver?
A taxicab driver?

I know! I'll be a mathematician,
Or a leading pediatrician.
I could even be a politician,
Or, I suppose, a busy beautician.

Woe is me!
Woe is me!
What to be?
What to be?

A snake charmer whose snake behaves?
A spelunker exploring caves?
An ironworker, brave and skilled,
With buildings or a bridge to build?

A traffic director, a building inspector?
A banker with money to spare?
A happy-faced clown, the mayor of some town?
A referee, honest and fair?

Or is there an orphan home somewhere
With children who'd need my loving care?
Or how many people would I reach
If I decide, instead, to teach?

Woe is me!
Woe is me!
What to be?
What to be?

Some jobs might bring me
Fame and treasure;
But others, perhaps,
Just simple pleasure.

How will I know which way to go,
The best road for me to take?
Though I know myself well,
I don't know how to tell
What's the best decision to make.

I must decide so many things
Within the years ahead:
Should I keep in step behind,
Or should I lead instead?

Woe is me!
Woe is me!
Will I see
What I'm to be?

While I'm pretending every day,
I'll find the things I like to play;
And when at last I'm fully grown,
I'll seek a place that's all my own.

For I still have a lot of time
To learn and grow and see;
And when I'm old enough to choose,
I'll know exactly
                WHAT TO BE.

About the Author:
Though the Baltimore, Maryland home of Meredith Powell is six hundred miles from the Marietta, Georgia home of her sister, Gail Yokubinas, these busy wives and mothers have managed to collaborate on this delightful book for children. Continuing to develop the creative talents encouraged by their parents, both women have found time to further their education. Mrs. Yokubinas is a full-time college student in the field of education and has been a substitute teacher in the Marietta and Cobb County school system in Georgia. Mrs. Powell, also a substitute teacher, has been enrolled in a creative development program and a commercial art course.

About the artist:
Mr. Mlodock is a graduate of the Art Institute of Chicago. Painting, his family and outdoor living are the most important things in his life, but he is a communications buff, as well. From videotape through photography, one of his greatest challenges is to create something out of nothing. He lives with his family in suburban Deerfield, Illinois.